Easy Dates Cookbook

50 Delicious Date Recipes; Simple Methods for Cooking with Dates

By
BookSumo Press

Published by
http://www.booksumo.com

LEGAL NOTES

Table of Contents

Cinnamon Clove
Pecan Cookies

🥣 Prep Time: 1 hr
🕐 Total Time: 1 hr 10 mins

Servings per Recipe: 36
Calories	156 kcal
Fat	7.8 g
Carbohydrates	20.4g
Protein	2.1 g
Cholesterol	29 mg
Sodium	77 mg

Ingredients

1 C. butter, softened
1 1/3 C. white sugar
3 eggs
3 C. sifted all-purpose flour
1 tsp baking soda
1/2 tsp ground cinnamon
1/4 tsp ground cloves

2 tsp water
1 1/2 C. chopped pitted dates
1 C. chopped pecans

Directions

1. In a large bowl, add the butter and sugar and beat till light and fluffy.
2. Add the eggs, one at a time and beat till well combined.
3. In another bowl, mix together the flour, baking soda, cinnamon and cloves.
4. Slowly, add the flour mixture into the butter mixture and mix till well combined.
5. In a small bowl, mix together the water and dates.
6. Add the date mixture and chopped pecans into the dough and mix well.
7. Refrigerate, covered for about 1 hour.
8. Set your oven to 375 degrees F and grease the cookie sheets.
9. With rounded spoonful, place the mixture onto the prepared cookie sheet.
10. Cook in the oven for about 8-10 minutes.
11. Remove from the oven and keep onto wire rack to cool in the pan for about 5 minutes.
12. Carefully, invert the cookies onto the wire rack to cool completely.

MIDDLE EASTERN
Inspired Date Cake

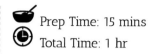 Prep Time: 15 mins

Total Time: 1 hr

Servings per Recipe: 12
Calories	366 kcal
Fat	16.7 g
Carbohydrates	53g
Protein	4.1 g
Cholesterol	65 mg
Sodium	253 mg

Ingredients

1 1/2 C. water
1 1/2 C. raisins
3/4 C. dates, pitted and chopped
1 tsp baking soda
1/2 C. butter
3/4 C. white sugar
2 eggs

1 tsp vanilla extract
1 1/2 C. all-purpose flour
1/4 tsp salt
4 tbsp butter
1/2 C. brown sugar
2 tbsp heavy cream
1/2 C. chopped walnuts

Directions

1. Set your oven to 350 degrees F before doing anything else and grease and flour a 9-inch square baking dish.
2. In a pan, add the water and raisins and bring to a boil.
3. Cook for about 5 minutes.
4. Remove from the heat and stir in the chopped dates and baking soda.
5. In a large bowl, add 1/2 C. of the butter and 3/4 C. of the white sugar and beat till light and fluffy.
6. Add the eggs, one at a time and beat till well combined.
7. Stir in the vanilla.
8. Add the flour, salt and date mixture and mix till well combined.
9. Transfer the mixture into the prepared baking dish.
10. Cook in the oven for about 45 minutes or till a toothpick inserted in the center comes out clean.
11. Remove the cake from the oven.
12. Now, set the broiler of your oven.
13. For topping in a pan, melt 4 tbsp of the butter.

14. Stir in the brown sugar, cream and chopped nuts and remove from the heat.
15. Spread the cream mixture over the warm cake and cook under the broiler for about 3 minutes.
16. Remove from the heat and keep onto wire rack to cool before serving.

4TH GRADER'S
Favorite Date Brownies

Prep Time: 20 mins
Total Time: 55 mins

Servings per Recipe: 24	
Calories	176 kcal
Fat	8.7 g
Carbohydrates	22g
Protein	3.6 g
Cholesterol	36 mg
Sodium	101 mg

Ingredients

30 graham crackers, crushed
1/3 C. butter, melted
1 (14 oz.) can sweetened condensed milk
3 eggs
1 1/2 tbsp vanilla extract
1 C. chopped walnuts

1 C. chopped dates

Directions

1. Set your oven to 350 degrees F before doing anything else and grease a 13x9-inch baking dish.
2. In a bowl, mix together the graham cracker crumbs and melted butter.
3. For the crust in the bottom of the prepared baking dish, place the mixture and press to smooth.
4. In a bowl, add the sweetened condensed milk, eggs and vanilla extract and beat till well combined.
5. Fold in the walnuts and dates.
6. Place the mixture into the prepared pie crust evenly.
7. Cook in the oven for about 35 minutes or till a toothpick inserted in the center comes out clean. a
8. Remove from the oven and keep aside to cool slightly.
9. Cut the warm brownie mixture into desired sized bars.

Sweet
Orient Dessert Rolls

Prep Time: 15 mins
Total Time: 4 hr

Servings per Recipe: 36
Calories	198 kcal
Fat	6.3 g
Carbohydrates	34.4g
Protein	2.3 g
Cholesterol	16 mg
Sodium	108 mg

Ingredients

1 C. shortening
1 C. white sugar
1 C. packed brown sugar
3 eggs
1 tsp vanilla extract
1 tbsp water
4 C. all-purpose flour

1 tsp baking soda
1 tsp salt
1 pound dates, pitted and chopped
1/2 C. white sugar
1 C. water

Directions

1. In a bowl, add the shortening, 1 C. of the white sugar and 1 C. of the brown sugar and beat till creamy.
2. Add the eggs, vanilla and 1 tbsp of water and beat till well combined.
3. In another bowl, sift together the flour, soda and salt twice.
4. Add the flour mixture into the sugar mixture and mix till a dough forms.
5. Divide the dough into 2-3 equal sized portions.
6. For the filling in a pan, add the dates, 1/2 C. of the white sugar and 1 C. of the water on low heat and cook till the mixture becomes smooth, stirring continuously.
7. Remove from the oven and keep aside to cool completely.
8. Roll each dough portion into 1/4-1/2 inch thick rectangles.
9. Spread the filling over each rectangle evenly and then, roll up like a jelly roll.
10. Cover the dough rectangles and refrigerate for about 2-3 hours.
11. Set your oven to 350 degrees F.
12. Cut each dough rectangle into 1/4-1/2-inch thick slices.
13. Cook in the oven for about 10-12 minutes.

TROPICAL ISLAND
Coconut Date Balls

Prep Time: 15 mins
Total Time: 45 mins

Servings per Recipe: 36	
Calories	69 kcal
Fat	3 g
Carbohydrates	10.6 g
Protein	0.9 g
Cholesterol	< 1 mg
Sodium	13 mg

Ingredients

1 C. dates, pitted and chopped
1 tsp water
1 C. chopped walnuts
2 egg white
1 C. packed brown sugar
1 tbsp butter
1 C. shredded coconut

Directions

1. Set your oven to 350 degrees F before doing anything else and grease the cookie sheets.
2. In a small pan, add the butter, water and dates on low heat and bring to a boil.
3. Remove from the heat and keep aside for 10 minutes.
4. In a bowl, add the date mixture, brown sugar and chopped nuts and mix well.
5. In a small bowl, add the egg whites and beat till stiff.
6. Fold the beaten egg whites into the date mixture.
7. Roll the dough into 2-inch balls and then coat with the shredded coconut evenly.
8. Arrange the dough balls onto the cookie sheets about-2 inch apart
9. Cook in the oven for about 12-15 minutes.
10. Remove from the oven and keep onto wire rack to cool completely.

4-Ingredient
Gorgonzola Date
Party Appetizer

Prep Time: 15 mins

Total Time: 15 mins

Servings per Recipe: 36

Calories	53 kcal
Fat	2.8 g
Carbohydrates	6.6g
Protein	1.2 g
Cholesterol	5 mg
Sodium	31 mg

Ingredients

13 oz. package cream cheese, softened
3 oz. crumbled Gorgonzola cheese
36 pitted dates
36 walnut pieces

Directions

1. In a bowl, mix together the cream cheese and Gorgonzola cheese.
2. Cut a slit in each date and spread them flat.
3. Spread cheese mixture into each date and top with a walnut piece.

FATHIA'S
Potluck Cake

Prep Time: 20 mins
Total Time: 1 hr 30 mins

Servings per Recipe: 12	
Calories	386 kcal
Fat	20.9 g
Carbohydrates	48.4g
Protein	4.2 g
Cholesterol	55 mg
Sodium	198 mg

Ingredients

1 C. dates, pitted and chopped
1 C. water
1/2 C. butter
1 C. white sugar
1 tsp baking soda
1 1/2 C. all-purpose flour
1 egg, beaten

1 tsp vanilla extract
1 C. chopped walnuts
1/4 C. butter
1/3 C. heavy cream
1/2 C. brown sugar

Directions

1. Set your oven to 350 degrees F before doing anything else and grease a 9x5-inch loaf pan.
2. In a pan, add the dates and water on medium heat and bring to a boil.
3. Add in 1/2 C. of the butter and 1 C. of the sugar and stir till melted completely.
4. Remove from the heat and stir in the baking soda.
5. Keep aside to cool for about 10 minutes.
6. In a large bowl, add the date mixture, flour, eggs and vanilla and mix till well combined.
7. Stir in the chopped walnuts.
8. Transfer the mixture into the prepared loaf pan.
9. Cook in the oven for about 50-60 minutes or till a toothpick inserted in the center comes out clean.
10. Remove from the oven and keep onto wire rack to cool in the pan for about 10 minutes.
11. Carefully, invert the cakes onto the wire rack to cool completely.
12. For the warm sauce in a pan add 1/4 C. of the butter, cream and brown sugar on medium heat and bring to a boil, stirring continuously.
13. Cut the cake into desired sized slices and serve with the warm sauce.

Rice Cereal
Lunch Box Circles

🥣 Prep Time: 10 mins
🕐 Total Time: 25 mins

Servings per Recipe: 24	
Calories	87 kcal
Fat	1.8 g
Carbohydrates	17.6 g
Protein	1 g
Cholesterol	17 mg
Sodium	45 mg

Ingredients

2 eggs, beaten
1 C. white sugar
1 C. chopped dates
1 tsp vanilla extract
1 tbsp butter
3 C. crispy rice cereal
1 C. flaked coconut

Directions

1. In a medium pan, add the eggs sugar and dates on medium heat and bring to a boil, stirring occasionally.
2. Boil for about 5 minutes, stirring occasionally.
3. Remove from the heat and immediately, stir in the butter and vanilla.
4. Stir in the crispy rice cereal.
5. With the buttered hands, make the walnut sized balls from the mixture.
6. Coat the balls with the coconut and serve.

VALENTINE'S
Day Pudding

Prep Time: 40 mins
Total Time: 1 hr 30 mins

Servings per Recipe: 12
Calories	551 kcal
Fat	32.7 g
Carbohydrates	64.4g
Protein	4.6 g
Cholesterol	124 mg
Sodium	335 mg

Ingredients

1 C. flour
1 tsp baking powder
2 1/2 oz. dark chocolate, grated
7 oz. chopped pitted dates
1 1/4 C. water
1 tsp baking soda
1/4 C. softened butter

3/4 C. superfine castor sugar
2 eggs
1 C. heavy cream
1 C. firmly packed brown sugar
1 C. butter
2 tbsp confectioners' sugar for dusting
3 C. vanilla ice cream

Directions

1. Set your oven to 350 degrees F before doing anything else and grease a 12 cups muffin pan.
2. In a bowl, mix together the flour, baking powder and chocolate.
3. In a pan, add the dates and water on high heat and bring to a boil.
4. Remove from the heat and stir in the baking soda.
5. Keep aside for about 5 minutes.
6. Transfer the mixture into a blender and pulse till smooth.
7. In a bowl, add 1/4 C. of the butter and superfine sugar and beat till light and fluffy.
8. Add the eggs, one at a time and beat till well combined.
9. Add the flour mixture and date puree and mix till well combined.
10. Transfer the mixture into the prepared muffin cups evenly.
11. Cook in the oven for about 25 minutes.
12. Meanwhile in a pan, add the cream, brown sugar, and 1 C. of the butter on medium-low heat and cook till the butter melts, stirring continuously.
13. After 25 minutes, remove the muffin pan from the oven and keep on the wire rack to cool for about 10 minutes.

14. Carefully, remove the puddings from the muffin cups and transfer onto a baking sheet.
15. Place about 2 tbsp of the sauce over each pudding.
16. Cook in the oven for about 5 minutes more.
17. In the bottom of dessert plates, place some of the sauce.
18. Arrange a pudding in each plate over the sauce and lightly dust with the confectioners' sugar.
19. Serve with a topping of the ice cream.

CREAMY
Apple Salad

Prep Time: 20 mins
Total Time: 1 hr 20 mins

Servings per Recipe: 4
Calories   415 kcal
Fat   31.8 g
Carbohydrates   34g
Protein   3.9 g
Cholesterol   46 mg
Sodium   205 mg

Ingredients

2 C. peeled, diced tart apples
1 tbsp white sugar
1 tsp lemon juice
1 pinch salt
1/2 C. chopped celery
1/2 C. chopped pitted dates
1/2 C. chopped walnuts

1/4 C. mayonnaise
1/2 C. heavy cream
1/4 C. maraschino cherries

Directions

1. In a serving bowl, mix together the apples, sugar, lemon juice, salt, celery, dates and walnuts.
2. In another bowl, add the cream and with an electric mixer, beat till it holds a peak.
3. Add the mayonnaise and stir to combine.
4. Gently fold in the apple mixture and cherries.
5. Refrigerate this salad for at least 1 hour to chill before serving.

Kale
Party Sampler

Prep Time: 30 mins
Total Time: 30 mins

Servings per Recipe: 8
Calories   291 kcal
Fat   9.6 g
Carbohydrates   51.7g
Protein   7 g
Cholesterol   0 mg
Sodium   25 mg

Ingredients

1 bunch kale, stems removed and
discarded
1 pound dates
1 C. whole roasted unsalted almonds

Directions

1. Tear all the kale leaf into 2 halves.
2. Split the dates in half and remove the pits.
3. Place an almond in each date half and wrap in a kale leaf half.
4. With a toothpick, pierce each leaf to keep wrapped.

CORN FLAKE
Cookies

Prep Time: 10 mins
Total Time: 30 mins

Servings per Recipe: 12
Calories	391 kcal
Fat	16.5 g
Carbohydrates	57.7g
Protein	4.4 g
Cholesterol	72 mg
Sodium	249 mg

Ingredients

2 1/2 C. all-purpose flour
1 tsp baking soda
1 C. butter
1/2 C. packed brown sugar
2 tsp vanilla extract
1 C. white sugar
2 eggs

1 C. dates, pitted and chopped
1 C. sugar frosted corn flake cereal

Directions

1. Set your oven to 350 degrees F before doing anything else.
2. In a small bowl, mix together the flour and baking soda.
3. In another bowl, add the butter, brown sugar, vanilla and white sugar and beat till creamy.
4. Add the eggs and beat till well combined.
5. Slowly, add the flour mixture and mix till well combined.
6. Fold in the dates.
7. With tsps of the mixture, make small balls and coat with the crushed corn flake cereal evenly.
8. Arrange the balls onto the ungreased cookie sheets in a single layer.
9. Cook in the oven for about 10-15 minutes.

Layla's
Cookies

Prep Time: 30 mins
Total Time: 45 mins

Servings per Recipe: 48
Calories   114 kcal
Fat   4.3 g
Carbohydrates   17.9g
Protein   1.5 g
Cholesterol   15 mg
Sodium   82 mg

Ingredients

1 1/2 C. chopped pitted dates
1/4 C. white sugar
1 pinch salt
3/4 C. orange juice
3/4 C. water
1 tsp orange zest
2/3 C. chopped pecans
3 1/2 C. all-purpose flour
1 1/2 tsp baking powder

1/4 tsp baking soda
3/4 tsp salt
3/4 C. butter, softened
1/2 C. white sugar
1 C. brown sugar
2 eggs
1 1/2 tsp vanilla extract
2 tsp orange zest

Directions

1. In a medium pan, add the dates, 1/4 C. of the sugar, a pinch of the salt, orange juice and water on medium heat and cook till the dates become soft, stirring continuously.
2. Remove from the heat and stir in 1 tsp of the orange zest and pecans.
3. Keep aside to cool completely.
4. After cooling, transfer the mixture in a food processor and pulse till the pecans are grounded finely.
5. In a bowl, sift together the flour, baking powder, baking soda and 3/4 tsp of the salt.
6. In another large bowl, add the butter, 1/2 C. of the white sugar and brown sugar and beat till smooth.
7. Add the eggs, one at a time and beat till well combined.
8. Stir in the vanilla and 2 tsp of the orange zest.
9. Add the flour mixture and mix till a smooth dough forms.
10. Divide the dough into thirds.
11. With a plastic wrap, cover the dough and refrigerate till firm.
12. Roll each dough third into a 1/4-inch in thick rectangle.

13. Spread 1/3 of the filling over each rectangle, leaving a 1-inch strip of dough uncovered on one of the long sides.
14. Starting at the edge opposite of the uncovered strip, roll the dough into jellyroll style and seal by pressing lightly.
15. With waxed paper, wrap the rolls and refrigerate till firm.
16. Set your oven to 350 degrees F and grease the cookie sheets.
17. Cut the chilled dough rolls into about 1/4-inch thick slices.
18. Place the slices onto the prepared cookie sheets about 2-inch apart.
19. Cook in the oven for about 12-15 minutes.
20. Remove from the oven and keep onto the wire rack to cool in the pan for about 5 minutes.
21. Carefully, invert the cookies onto the wire rack to cool completely.

Buttermilk
Date Muffins

Prep Time: 15 mins
Total Time: 35 mins

Servings per Recipe: 12
Calories	218 kcal
Fat	8.4 g
Carbohydrates	33.5g
Protein	3.1 g
Cholesterol	36 mg
Sodium	207 mg

Ingredients

1 thin skinned orange, cut into eighths and seeded
1 egg
1/2 C. buttermilk
1/2 C. chopped pitted dates
1/2 C. butter
1 3/4 C. all-purpose flour

3/4 C. white sugar
1 tsp baking soda
1 tsp baking powder
1 pinch salt
1 tsp ground cloves
1 tsp ground ginger

Directions

1. Set your oven to 400 degrees F before doing anything else and grease a 12 cups muffin pan.
2. In a blender, add the orange pieces, egg, buttermilk, dates and butter and pulse till a thick and fairly smooth mixture forms.
3. Transfer the mixture into a large bowl.
4. In another bowl, mix together the flour, sugar, baking soda, baking powder, salt, cloves and ginger.
5. Add the flour mixture into the orange mixture and with a wooden spoon gently, fold to combine.
6. Transfer the mixture into the prepared muffin cups evenly.
7. Cook in the oven for about 20 minutes or till a toothpick inserted in the center comes out clean.
8. Remove from the oven and keep onto the wire rack to cool in the muffin pan for about 5 minutes.
9. Carefully, invert the muffins onto the wire rack to cool completely.

GOAT CHEESE
Appetizers

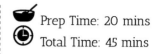 Prep Time: 20 mins
Total Time: 45 mins

Servings per Recipe: 20
Calories	249 kcal
Fat	22.2 g
Carbohydrates	11.8g
Protein	4.5 g
Cholesterol	5 mg
Sodium	95 mg

Ingredients

20 pitted dates
1/4 C. goat cheese
20 oz. pecans
10 slices turkey bacon, cut in half
1/2 C. balsamic vinegar
1 tbsp white sugar

Directions

1. Set your oven to 350 degrees F before doing anything else.
2. Split the dates in half and remove the pits.
3. Stuff each date with about 1/2 tsp of the goat cheese.
4. Place 1 pecan over each date and gently, press into the cheese.
5. Wrap each date with a halved bacon slice and arrange onto a baking sheet.
6. Cook in the oven for about 15-20 minutes.
7. In a pan, add the balsamic vinegar and sugar on medium heat and cook till the mixture becomes thick, stirring continuously.
8. Serve the dates with a topping of the sugar mixture.

Moroccan
Couscous from Marrakesh

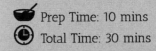 Prep Time: 10 mins

Total Time: 30 mins

Servings per Recipe: 2
Calories	594 kcal
Fat	10.6 g
Carbohydrates	111.9 g
Protein	18 g
Cholesterol	0 mg
Sodium	315 mg

Ingredients

1 tbsp olive oil
1 medium onion, chopped
2 whole star anise pods
salt to taste
3 cloves garlic, peeled and chopped
1/2 red bell pepper, chopped
2 dried hot red peppers, diced

1/2 tsp ground black pepper
4 large fresh mushrooms, chopped
1 tbsp lemon juice
1/4 C. chopped dates
1 tsp ground cinnamon
1 C. uncooked couscous
1 1/2 C. vegetable stock

Directions

1. In a medium pan, heat the oil on medium heat and sauté the onion till tender.
2. Stir in the anise pods, salt, garlic, red bell pepper, dried hot red peppers and black pepper and cook till the vegetables become tender.
3. Stir in the mushrooms, lemon juice, dates and cinnamon reduce the heat to low.
4. Simmer for about 10 minutes.
5. In a medium pan, add the couscous and vegetable stock and bring to a boil.
6. Reduce the heat to low and simmer, covered for about 3-5 minutes.
7. Remove from the heat and with a fork, fluff the couscous.
8. Add the vegetables and stir to combine.
9. Serve immediately.

STRONG BREWED
Breakfast Bread

Prep Time: 20 mins
Total Time: 1 hr 20 mins

Servings per Recipe: 8
Calories	363 kcal
Fat	13.5 g
Carbohydrates	58.7g
Protein	5 g
Cholesterol	31 mg
Sodium	479 mg

Ingredients

1 C. chopped pitted dates
1 tsp baking soda
1 C. strong brewed coffee
2 tbsp butter, softened
1 C. white sugar
1 egg
1 tsp vanilla extract

1 1/2 C. all-purpose flour
1 tsp salt
1 C. chopped pecans

Directions

1. Set your oven to 350 degrees F before doing anything else and line the bottom of a greased 8x4-inch loaf pan with the parchment paper.
2. In a small bowl, add the dates and sprinkle with the baking soda.
3. In another small pan, add the coffee and bring to a gentle boil.
4. Remove from the heat and place the coffee over the dates and soda.
5. In a bowl, add the butter, sugar and egg and beat till well combined.
6. Stir in the vanilla.
7. Add the flour and salt and mix till well combined.
8. Fold in the pecans and date mixture.
9. Transfer the mixture into the prepared loaf pan evenly.
10. Cook in the oven for about 1 hour or till the top of the loaf springs back when lightly touched.
11. Remove from the oven and keep onto the wire rack to cool in the pan for about 5 minutes.
12. Carefully, invert the cookies onto the wire rack to cool completely.

New York
Date Squares

Prep Time: 25 mins
Total Time: 50 mins

Servings per Recipe: 12
Calories	363 kcal
Fat	12.5 g
Carbohydrates	63.7g
Protein	3.7 g
Cholesterol	31 mg
Sodium	217 mg

Ingredients

1 1/2 C. rolled oats
1 1/2 C. sifted pastry flour
1/4 tsp salt
3/4 tsp baking soda
1 C. packed brown sugar
3/4 C. butter, softened
3/4 pound pitted dates, diced

1 C. water
1/3 C. packed brown sugar
1 tsp lemon juice

Directions

1. Set your oven to 350 degrees F before doing anything else.
2. In a large bowl, mix together the oats, pastry flour, salt, 1 C. of the brown sugar and baking soda.
3. Add the butter and mix till a crumbly mixture forms.
4. Place half of the mixture in the bottom of a 9-inch square baking dish and press to smooth.
5. In a small pan, add the dates, water, and 1/3 C. of the brown sugar on medium heat and bring to a boil.
6. Cook till the mixture becomes thick, stirring continuously.
7. Stir in the lemon juice and remove from the heat.
8. Place the filling over the base evenly.
9. Top with the remaining crumb mixture and slightly, press to smooth the surface.
10. Cook in the oven for about 20-25 minutes.
11. Remove from the oven and keep aside to cool completely before cutting.
12. Cut into desired sized squares and serve.

FLAX SEED
Fibrous Bread

Prep Time: 10 mins
Total Time: 1 hr 5 mins

Servings per Recipe: 10
Calories	263 kcal
Fat	10.5 g
Carbohydrates	42.6g
Protein	6.7 g
Cholesterol	37 mg
Sodium	218 mg

Ingredients

1/2 C. flax seed
3 bananas, mashed
1/4 C. vegetable oil
1/2 C. white sugar
2 eggs
1 1/2 C. all-purpose flour
1/2 tsp baking powder

1/2 tsp baking soda
1/2 tsp salt
1/4 C. flax seed
1/2 C. chopped pitted dates

Directions

1. Set your oven to 350 degrees F before doing anything else and lightly, grease an 8x4-inch loaf pan.
2. In a food processor, grind 1/2 C. of the flax seeds.
3. In a large bowl, add the banana, oil, sugar and eggs and beat trill well combined.
4. In another bowl, mix together the flour, baking powder, baking soda, salt, ground flax seeds and 1/4 C. of the whole flax seeds.
5. Slowly, add the flour mixture into the banana mixture and mix till well combined.
6. Fold in the dates.
7. Transfer the mixture into the prepared loaf pan evenly.
8. Cook in the oven for about 55-60 minutes or till a toothpick inserted in the center comes out clean.
9. Remove from the oven and keep onto the wire rack to cool in the pan for about 5 minutes.
10. Carefully, invert the cookies onto the wire rack to cool completely.

Spicy Mediterranean
Meatloaf

🥣 Prep Time: 20 mins
🕐 Total Time: 1 hr 30 mins

Servings per Recipe: 8
Calories   291 kcal
Fat   15.1 g
Carbohydrates   19.4g
Protein   20 g
Cholesterol   87 mg
Sodium   306 mg

Ingredients

5 Poblano peppers
cooking spray
12 pitted Medjool dates
20 oz. -lean ground beef
5 oz. goat cheese
1/4 C. barbeque sauce
1/4 C. plain bread crumbs

1 egg
2 tbsp barbeque sauce

Directions

1. Set the broiler of your oven and arrange oven rack about 6-inches from the heating element.
2. Arrange the peppers onto a baking sheet and cook under the broiler for about 5-10 minutes per side.
3. Remove from the oven and immediately, transfer the peppers into a bowl of the chilled water for about 10 minutes.
4. Drain the peppers and peel the blackened skin, the remove the seeds.
5. Set your oven to 350 degrees F and grease a 9x5-inch loaf pan with the cooking spray.
6. In a food processor, add the peppers and dates and pulse till well combined.
7. In a bowl, add the date mixture, ground beef, goat cheese, 1/4 C. barbecue sauce, bread crumbs and egg and mix till well combined.
8. Transfer the mixture into the prepared loaf pan evenly.
9. Place about 2 tbsp of the barbecue sauce over the meat mixture evenly.
10. Cook in the oven for about 1 hour.

AN ISRAELI
Bittersweet Treat

Prep Time: 15 mins
Total Time: 1 hr 15 mins

Servings per Recipe: 25
Calories   86 kcal
Fat   4.2 g
Carbohydrates   11.7g
Protein   1 g
Cholesterol   < 1 mg
Sodium   2 mg

Ingredients

8 oz. bittersweet chocolate, chopped
25 pitted Medjool dates
25 pecan halves
2 tbsp sweetened shredded coconut
(optional)

Directions

1. In a microwave safe bowl, add the chocolate and microwave for about 2 minutes, stirring after every 30 seconds.
2. Remove from the microwave and stir till smooth.
3. Line a baking sheet with a piece of the foil.
4. Stuff each date with a pecan half and arrange onto the prepared baking sheet.
5. Drizzle with the melted chocolate and sprinkle with the coconut.
6. Freeze for about 1 hour before serving.

North African COUSCOUS

Prep Time: 10 mins
Total Time: 1 hr

Servings per Recipe: 4
Calories	417 kcal
Fat	17.5 g
Carbohydrates	52.7g
Protein	13.8 g
Cholesterol	18 mg
Sodium	918 mg

Ingredients

2 tbsp olive oil, divided
1/2 onion, chopped
1 C. pearl Israeli couscous
1 C. chicken broth
1 C. chopped cubed cooked chicken
1/2 C. chopped pitted dates
1/2 C. chopped dry-roasted almonds

1/4 C. chopped pitted green olives
1/4 C. freshly chopped parsley
salt and ground black pepper to taste

Directions

1. In a skillet, heat 1 tbsp olive oil on medium-low heat and cook the onion for about 30 minutes, stirring occasionally.
2. Stir in the couscous and increase the heat to medium.
3. Cook for about 5 minutes, stirring continuously.
4. Place the broth over the couscous mixture and bring to a boil.
5. Reduce the heat and simmer, covered for about 5-10 minutes.
6. In a small skillet, heat remaining 1 tbsp of the olive oil on medium heat and cook the cook for about 5 to 7 minutes until fully done.
7. In the pan of couscous, add the chicken, dates, almonds, olives, parsley, salt and pepper and cook for about 2-3 minutes.

MANHATTAN
Fruit Bars

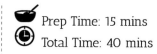

Prep Time: 15 mins
Total Time: 40 mins

Servings per Recipe: 24
Calories	205 kcal
Fat	7 g
Carbohydrates	34.5g
Protein	2.3 g
Cholesterol	0 mg
Sodium	57 mg

Ingredients

1 C. dates, pitted and chopped
1 3/4 C. drained stewed apricots
1/2 C. white sugar
2 tbsp apricot nectar
3/4 C. shortening, melted
1 C. packed brown sugar
2 C. all-purpose flour

1 tsp baking soda
2 C. quick cooking oats
1 tsp vanilla extract

Directions

1. For filling in a pan, add the dates, drained cooked apricots, white sugar and apricot juice and cook for about 3 minutes.
2. For the crust in a bowl, add the melted shortening, brown sugar, all-purpose flour, baking soda, quick cooking oats and vanilla and mix till well combined.
3. In the bottom of a well-greased 12x9x2-inch baking dish, place half of the crust mixture and press to smooth.
4. Place the filling over the crust.
5. Top with the remaining crumb mixture and slightly, press to smooth the surface.
6. Cook in the oven for about 30 minutes.

Country
Squash Stuffed

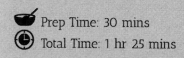 Prep Time: 30 mins

Total Time: 1 hr 25 mins

Servings per Recipe: 4
Calories	232 kcal
Fat	2.3 g
Carbohydrates	53.8g
Protein	5.5 g
Cholesterol	5 mg
Sodium	137 mg

Ingredients

2 slices turkey bacon, chopped
1 onion, chopped
2/3 C. chopped dates
1/2 tsp dried oregano
1/2 tsp dried basil
2 tbsp chicken stock
1 butternut squash

Directions

1. Set your oven to 375 degrees F before doing anything else.
2. Heat a large skillet on medium-high heat and cook the beef for about 10 minutes.
3. Transfer the bacon onto a paper towel lined plate to drain.
4. Drain the grease from the skillet, leaving about 2 tsp inside the skillet.
5. In the same skillet, sauté the onion in the bacon grease for about 5 minutes.
6. Stir in the cooked bacon, dates, oregano, basil and chicken stock and remove from the heat.
7. Cut the top and stem of the squash and scoop out the seeds and stringy pulp.
8. Cut out the small button at the bottom of the squash.
9. Stuff the squash cavity with the date filling and cover with the top of the squash.
10. Arrange the squash into a baking dish and, add about 1/2-inch of the water.
11. With a piece of the foil, cover the baking dish and cook in the oven for about 40-60 minutes.
12. Cut the squash into the wedges and serve.

LEMONY
Date Crisps

Prep Time: 20 mins
Total Time: 2 hr 20 mins

Servings per Recipe: 24
Calories	251 kcal
Fat	12.2 g
Carbohydrates	35.5g
Protein	3 g
Cholesterol	31 mg
Sodium	89 mg

Ingredients

4 C. chopped pitted honey dates
3/4 C. orange juice
1/2 tsp lemon juice
2 C. whole wheat flour
2 C. quick-cooking oats
3/4 C. brown sugar
1/2 tsp baking powder

1/2 tsp baking soda
1/2 tsp salt
1 1/2 C. unsalted butter, melted and cooled

Directions

1. Set your oven to 325 degrees F before doing anything else and line an 11x9-inch greased baking dish with the parchment paper.
2. In a large pan, add the dates, orange juice and lemon juice on medium-low heat and cook for about 6 minutes, stirring occasionally.
3. In a large bowl, mix together the whole wheat flour, oats, brown sugar, baking powder, baking soda and salt.
4. In the bottom of the prepared baking dish, place half of the oat mixture and press to smooth.
5. Place the date mixture over the oat mixture evenly.
6. Top with the remaining crumb mixture and slightly, press to smooth the surface.
7. Cook in the oven for about 20 minutes.
8. Remove from the oven and keep onto the wire rack to cool in the pan for about 30 minutes.
9. Refrigerate for about 1 hour.
10. Cut into desired sized squares and serve.

November
Potato Sweet Casserole

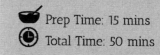

🥣 Prep Time: 15 mins
🕐 Total Time: 50 mins

Servings per Recipe: 6
Calories	780 kcal
Fat	46.5 g
Carbohydrates	86.2g
Protein	9.7 g
Cholesterol	157 mg
Sodium	291 mg

Ingredients

cooking spray
2 C. mashed sweet potatoes
1 C. pitted, chopped dates
3/4 C. brown sugar
2 eggs, beaten
1/2 C. butter, melted
1/2 C. heavy whipping cream
1 tsp vanilla extract

1/2 tsp ground cinnamon
1/2 tsp ground nutmeg
1 C. granola cereal
1/2 C. brown sugar
1/2 C. chopped pecans
1/3 C. all-purpose flour
1/3 C. butter, melted

Directions

1. Set your oven to 425 degrees F before doing anything else and grease a 2-quart baking dish with the cooking spray.
2. In a bowl, add the sweet potatoes, dates, 3/4 C. of the brown sugar, eggs, 1/2 C. of the melted butter, cream, vanilla extract, cinnamon and nutmeg and mix till well combined.
3. Transfer the mixture into the prepared baking dish evenly.
4. Cook in the oven for about 20 minutes.
5. In a bowl, add the granola cereal, 1/2 C. of the brown sugar, pecans and flour and mix till a crumbly mixture forms.
6. Ass about 1/3 C. of the melted butter into granola mixture and mix till well combined.
7. Remove the baking dish from the oven and spread the granola mixture over the sweet potatoes evenly.
8. Cook in the oven for about 15 minutes.

LONDON
Dates Sampler

Prep Time: 1 hr
Total Time: 1 hr 45 mins

Servings per Recipe: 48

Calories	130 kcal
Fat	4.8 g
Carbohydrates	21.5g
Protein	1.2 g
Cholesterol	23 mg
Sodium	53 mg

Ingredients

24 pecan halves, split lengthwise
48 pitted dates
6 tbsp butter, softened
1 C. packed brown sugar
3 egg yolks
2 1/4 C. all-purpose flour
3/4 tsp baking soda

3/4 tsp baking powder
1 C. sour cream
6 tbsp butter
2 1/4 C. confectioners' sugar
1 1/2 tsp vanilla extract
5 tsp milk

Directions

1. Set your oven to 375 degrees F before doing anything else and line the baking sheets with the parchment papers.
2. Stuff each date with a piece of the pecan.
3. In a bowl, add 6 tbsp of the butter and brown sugar and beat till creamy.
4. Add the egg yolks and beat till well combined.
5. In another bowl, mix together the flour, baking soda and baking powder.
6. Slowly, add the flour mixture into the butter mixture, alternating with sour cream and mix till well combined.
7. Add the dates and stir to combine with the dough.
8. With about 2 tbsp, pick up 1 date with enough dough to cover and arrange onto the prepared baking sheets.
9. Cook in the oven for about 7-9 minutes.
10. Remove from the oven and keep aside to cool completely before serving.
11. In a pan, melt 6 tbsp of the butter for about 2 minutes.
12. Add the confectioners' sugar, vanilla extract and milk and mix till the frosting becomes smooth.
13. Immediately, spread warm frosting over each date cookie and keep aside till set.

Sandy Beach
Bread

🥣 Prep Time: 20 mins
🕐 Total Time: 1 hr 20 mins

Servings per Recipe: 12
Calories   224 kcal
Fat   7.5 g
Carbohydrates   38.3g
Protein   3.2 g
Cholesterol   16 mg
Sodium   332 mg

Ingredients

1 C. chopped dates
3/4 C. boiling water
1 tsp baking soda
1/4 C. margarine
3/4 C. chocolate chips
1 egg
1/2 C. white sugar

3/4 tsp salt
1 tsp vanilla extract
1 3/4 C. all-purpose flour
1 tsp baking powder

Directions

1. In a small bowl, mix together the dates, boiling water and baking soda and keep aside to cool completely.
2. In a bowl over a pan of simmering water, melt the chocolate chips and margarine till smooth, stirring continuously.
3. In a bowl, add the egg and beat well.
4. Stir in the sugar, salt and vanilla.
5. Stir in the melted chocolate and date mixtures.
6. In another bowl, mix together the flour and baking powder.
7. Add the flour mixture into the date mixture and mix till just combined.
8. Set your oven to 350 degrees F before doing anything else and grease a 9x5-inch loaf pan.
9. Scrape the mixture into the prepared loaf pan and keep aside for about 20 minutes.
10. Cook in the oven for about 1 hour or till a toothpick inserted in the center comes out clean.
11. Remove from the oven and keep onto the wire rack to cool in the pan for about 10 minutes.
12. Carefully, invert the loaf onto the wire rack to cool completely.
13. For better taste, preserve this loaf in refrigerate by wrapping in a piece of the foil for about overnight.

HOW TO MAKE
a Date Frosting

Prep Time: 5 mins
Total Time: 5 mins

Servings per Recipe: 15

Calories	220 kcal
Fat	5.3 g
Carbohydrates	43.3g
Protein	1.4 g
Cholesterol	15 mg
Sodium	47 mg

Ingredients

1/3 C. butter, softened
2/3 C. sweetened condensed milk
3 tbsp orange juice concentrate
1/2 tsp orange zest
3 1/2 C. confectioners' sugar
3/4 C. pitted dates

Directions

1. In a bowl, add the butter, condensed milk, orange juice concentrate and orange zest and beat till smooth.
2. Slowly, add the confectioners' sugar and beat till a spreadable consistency is acquired.
3. Frost the cake and serve with a decoration of the dates.

Carolina
Mayo Cake

🥣 Prep Time: 15 mins
🕐 Total Time: 1 hr

Servings per Recipe: 18
Calories	340 kcal
Fat	19.5 g
Carbohydrates	40.5g
Protein	3.1 g
Cholesterol	29 mg
Sodium	251 mg

Ingredients

1 C. dates, pitted and chopped
2 tsp baking soda
1 C. boiling water
2 C. all-purpose flour
1 C. white sugar
1 C. mayonnaise
1 C. chopped walnuts

1/4 C. water
1 egg, beaten
1 C. white sugar
1/2 C. butter
3/4 tsp lemon zest
3 tbsp lemon juice

Directions

1. Set your oven to 350 degrees F before doing anything else and lightly, grease a 15x9-inch cake pan.
2. In a large bowl, mix together the dates, 1 tsp of the soda and boiling water and keep aside to cool completely.
3. Add the flour, 1 C. of the sugar, mayonnaise and remaining 1 tsp of the soda and with an electric mixer, beat on medium speed till well combined. Stir in nuts.
4. Transfer the mixture into prepared pan evenly.
5. Cook in the oven for about 45 minutes or till a toothpick inserted in the center comes out clean.
6. Meanwhile for the lemon sauce in a medium pan, mix together the beaten egg and 1/4 C. of the water on medium heat.
7. Add 1 C. of the sugar, butter, lemon peel and juice and bring to a boil, stirring continuously.
8. Spread the sauce over the warm cake and serve.

CASABLANCA
Chicken Sampler

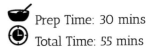 Prep Time: 30 mins

Total Time: 55 mins

Servings per Recipe: 2
Calories	447 kcal
Fat	18.1 g
Carbohydrates	36.3g
Protein	36.7 g
Cholesterol	97 mg
Sodium	88 mg

Ingredients

1/4 C. dates, pitted and chopped
1 small apple - peeled, cored, and chopped
2 tbsp chopped dried apricots
2 tbsp raisins
1 tbsp grated orange zest
1 tbsp orange juice

1/4 tsp cayenne pepper
1/4 tsp ground cardamom
1/4 tsp ground mace
26 oz.) skinless, boneless chicken breast halves
2 tbsp vegetable oil

Directions

1. Set your oven to 350 degrees F before doing anything else.
2. In a bowl, add the dates, apple, apricots, raisins, orange zest, orange juice, cayenne pepper, cardamom, and mace and mix till well combined.
3. Arrange 2 heavy plastic sheets onto a smooth surface.
4. Place the chicken breasts between the plastic sheets and with a meat mallet, pound firmly into 1/4-inch thickness.
5. Place the fruit filling over the flattened breasts and roll up, tucking in the ends.
6. Secure the breast roll with the toothpicks.
7. In an oven proof skillet, heat the vegetable oil on medium-high heat and cook the chicken breast rolls for about 5 minutes.
8. Transfer the skillet in the oven and cook in the oven for about 20-25 minutes.

Spicy
South Indian Chutney

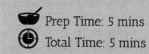 Prep Time: 5 mins

Total Time: 5 mins

Servings per Recipe: 8
Calories	17 kcal
Fat	0.1 g
Carbohydrates	4.3g
Protein	0.2 g
Cholesterol	0 mg
Sodium	291 mg

Ingredients

5 pitted whole dates
1/2 C. water
1 tbsp tamarind concentrate
1 tbsp cayenne pepper
1 tsp salt

Directions

1. In a blender, add all the ingredients and pulse till smooth.

STUFFED DATES
Barcelona Style

Prep Time: 20 mins
Total Time: 50 mins

Servings per Recipe: 12
Calories	398 kcal
Fat	40 g
Carbohydrates	8.4g
Protein	3.1 g
Cholesterol	22 mg
Sodium	121 mg

Ingredients

1 beef sausage link
12 pitted dates
3 slices turkey bacon, cut into fourths
2 C. vegetable oil for frying (optional)
1 egg, beaten (optional)
1 tsp water (optional)
1/4 C. all-purpose flour (optional)

Directions

1. Cut the ends off of the sausage and then cut into 12 equal sized cubes.
2. Stuff the dates with a piece of the sausage and wrap with a piece of the bacon.
3. Secure each date with the toothpicks.
4. Heat a skillet on medium-high heat.
5. Place the dates in the skillet, seam side down of the bacon and fry till the bacon becomes golden brown from both sides.
6. You can also fry these wrapped dates in another manner too.
7. In a deep-fryer, heat the oil to 375 degrees F.
8. In a small bowl, add the egg and water and beat till well combined.
9. Roll the dates into the flour and then dip into the egg and immediately fry in the hot oil for about 2 minutes per side.
10. Transfer onto a paper towel lined plate to drain.
11. Serve immediately.

Arabian Dream
Cookies

🥣 Prep Time: 15 mins
🕐 Total Time: 45 mins

Servings per Recipe: 18
Calories	117 kcal
Fat	2.3 g
Carbohydrates	23.2g
Protein	2 g
Cholesterol	0 mg
Sodium	32 mg

Ingredients

1 C. all-purpose flour
1/2 tsp baking powder
3 egg whites
1 pinch salt
1 C. white sugar
2/3 C. dates, pitted and chopped
1/2 C. chopped walnuts
1/3 C. confectioners' sugar for decoration

Directions

1. Set your oven to 375 degrees F before doing anything else and lightly, grease a 9-inch square baking dish.
2. In a bowl, mix together the flour and baking powder.
3. In another large, dry glass bowl, add the egg whites and salt and beat till foamy.
4. Slowly, add the sugar and beat till the mixture becomes stiff but not dry.
5. Slowly, add the flour mixture and gently, stir to combine.
6. Now, fold in the dates and nuts.
7. Transfer the mixture into the prepared baking dish evenly.
8. Cook in the oven for about 20-30 minutes.
9. Remove from the oven and cool in the pan onto a wire rack till just cool enough to handle.
10. Cut into finger-sized lengths and then, roll between palms to form the logs.
11. Coat each log with the confectioners' sugar evenly.
12. Keep aside onto wire rack to cool completely on wire rack.

SWEET
Date Canes

Prep Time: 10 mins
Total Time: 40 mins

Servings per Recipe: 12

Calories	154 kcal
Fat	4.1 g
Carbohydrates	29.2g
Protein	1.8 g
Cholesterol	21 mg
Sodium	89 mg

Ingredients

1/2 C. all-purpose flour
1/2 tsp baking powder
1/4 tsp salt
1 egg
1/3 C. white sugar
1 tbsp butter, melted and cooled
1 C. dates, pitted and chopped

1/4 C. chopped walnuts
1 tbsp milk
1 tbsp butter
1 C. confectioners' sugar
1 tsp lemon juice
1/2 tsp lemon zest

Directions

1. Set your oven to 325 degrees F before doing anything else and lightly, grease an 8x8-inch baking dish.
2. In a bowl, sift together the flour, baking powder and salt.
3. In another bowl, add the egg and sugar and slowly, beat till creamy.
4. Add 1 tbsp of the butter and beat till well combined.
5. Stir in the dates and walnuts.
6. Slowly, add the flour mixture and mix till well combined.
7. Transfer the mixture into the prepared baking dish evenly.
8. Cook in the oven for about 25-30 minutes.
9. Remove from the oven and keep onto the wire rack to cool completely.
10. For the glaze in a pan, add 1 tbsp of the milk, 1 tbsp of the butter, 1 C. of the confectioners' sugar, 1 tsp of the lemon juice and 1/2 tsp of the grated lemon rind on low heat and cook till well combined, stirring continuously.
11. Remove from the heat and keep aside to cool slightly.
12. Spread the warm glaze over the baked mixture and cut into 24 sticks.

Bran and Cinnamon
Date Muffins

🥣 Prep Time: 10 mins
🕐 Total Time: 30 mins

Servings per Recipe: 12
Calories   210 kcal
Fat   4.1 g
Carbohydrates   40.3g
Protein   3.5 g
Cholesterol   16 mg
Sodium   371 mg

Ingredients

2 1/8 C. all-purpose flour
2 tbsp baking powder
1/2 tsp ground cinnamon
1/2 tsp salt
1/2 C. sugar
1/2 C. reduced-calorie margarine
1 egg

3 medium ripe bananas, mashed
1 1/2 tsp vanilla extract
3/4 C. bran flakes cereal
12 dates, pitted and chopped

Directions

1. Set your oven to 400 degrees F before doing anything else and line a 12 cups muffin pan with the paper liners.
2. In a bowl, sift together the flour, baking powder, cinnamon and salt.
3. In another bowl, add the sugar, margarine and egg and with an electric mixer, beat till light and fluffy.
4. Add the bananas, vanilla, cereal and dates and stir to combine.
5. Add the flour mixture and mix till just combined.
6. Transfer the mixture into the prepared muffin cups about 2/3 of full.
7. Cook in the oven for about 20-25 minutes or till a toothpick inserted in the center comes out clean.
8. Remove from the oven and keep onto the wire rack to cool in the pan for about 10 minutes.
9. Carefully, invert the muffins onto the wire rack to cool completely.

DATE
Candy Snake

Prep Time: 10 mins
Total Time: 40 mins

Servings per Recipe: 11
Calories	359 kcal
Fat	9.1 g
Carbohydrates	69.6g
Protein	4.1 g
Cholesterol	7 mg
Sodium	26 mg

Ingredients

3 C. white sugar
1 C. evaporated milk
1 C. dates, pitted and chopped
1 C. chopped nuts

Directions

1. Grease a 15x12-inch piece of the foil and dust with the confectioners' sugar generously.
2. In a pan, add the sugar and evaporated milk on medium-high heat and heat to 235 degrees F, stirring continuously.
3. Stir in the dates and nuts and remove from the heat.
4. Keep aside to cool completely.
5. Make about 1-1/2-inch roll from the candy and wrap into the prepared piece of the foil.
6. Refrigerate till firm.
7. Dip the knife in hot water and cut into thin slices.

Grandma's
4-Ingredient Rice Pudding

Prep Time: 10 mins
Total Time: 30 mins

Servings per Recipe: 6
Calories   192 kcal
Fat   1.8 g
Carbohydrates   40.5g
Protein   4.6 g
Cholesterol   7 mg
Sodium   34 mg

Ingredients

2 C. cooked white rice
2 C. milk
3 tbsp white sugar
15 dates, pitted and chopped

Directions

1. In a food processor, add the rice and pulse till chopped roughly but not pureed.
2. Transfer the rice into a pan with the milk, sugar and dates on low heat and cook for about 20 minutes, stirring occasionally.
3. This pudding can be served warm or cold as well.

WINDING RIDGE
Cauliflower

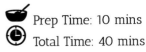
Prep Time: 10 mins
Total Time: 40 mins

Servings per Recipe: 4
Calories	255 kcal
Fat	17.5 g
Carbohydrates	23.3g
Protein	6.2 g
Cholesterol	31 mg
Sodium	46 mg

Ingredients

1 head cauliflower, cut into florets
salt and ground black pepper to taste
1/4 C. unsalted butter
1/3 C. pine nuts
1/2 C. coarsely chopped Medjool dates
1 clove garlic, minced

Directions

1. Set your oven to 425 degrees F before doing anything else.
2. Place the cauliflower florets onto a baking sheet and sprinkle with the salt and pepper.
3. Cook in the oven for about 10 minutes.
4. Stir the cauliflower and cook in the oven for about 20 minutes more.
5. In a small skillet, melt the butter on medium-low heat and cook the pine nuts for about 5 minutes.
6. Add the dates and garlic and cook for about 2-3 minutes.
7. Season with the salt and remove from the heat.
8. In a serving bowl, place the hot cauliflower and pine nut mixture and toss to coat.
9. This cauliflower can be served warm or at room temperature as well.

3-Ingredient
Dates for February

Prep Time: 1 hr
Total Time: 1 hr

Servings per Recipe: 24
Calories	70 kcal
Fat	1 g
Carbohydrates	14.7g
Protein	2 g
Cholesterol	< 1 mg
Sodium	51 mg

Ingredients

18 oz. package fat-free cream cheese, softened
1/4 C. finely chopped walnuts
28 oz. packages whole pitted dates

Directions

1. In a small bowl, mix together the cream cheese and walnuts.
2. With a small sharp knife, cut one side of each date lengthwise to create an opening.
3. Carefully, place the cream cheese mixture into the center of each date.
4. Pinch the dates to secure the filling.
5. In a plate, place the dates, cut sides down and serve.

CHIA, ZUCCHINI
Applesauce, Muffins

🥣 Prep Time: 15 mins
🕐 Total Time: 1 hr

Servings per Recipe: 12
Calories	224 kcal
Fat	14.8 g
Carbohydrates	21.3g
Protein	4.8 g
Cholesterol	0 mg
Sodium	205 mg

Ingredients

1/4 C. chia seeds
1 C. water
1 C. cashew flour
1/4 C. ground flax seed
2 tbsp coconut flour
2 tbsp tapioca starch
1 tbsp ground cinnamon

1 tsp baking soda
1/2 tsp salt
1 C. chopped dates
1 C. chopped walnuts
1 C. shredded zucchini
1/3 C. applesauce
2 tbsp coconut oil, melted
1 fluid oz. liquid stevia

Directions

1. Set your oven to 375 degrees F before doing anything else and line a 12 cups muffin pan with the paper liners.
2. In a large bowl, add the water and soak the chia seeds for about 5-10 minutes.
3. In a bowl, mix together the flax seed, flours, tapioca starch, cinnamon, baking soda and salt.
4. In another bowl, add the chia seed mixture, dates, walnuts, zucchini, applesauce, coconut oil and stevia and mix till well combined.
5. Add the date mixture into the flour mixture and nix till just combined.
6. Transfer the mixture into the prepared muffin cups evenly.
7. Cook in the oven for about 30-35 minutes or till a toothpick inserted in the center comes out clean.
8. Remove from the oven and keep onto the wire rack to cool in the pan for about 10 minutes.
9. Carefully, invert the muffins onto the wire rack to cool completely.

Chicken Breast
with Couscous
(Full Mediterranean
Dinner)

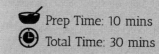

Prep Time: 10 mins
Total Time: 30 mins

Servings per Recipe: 2

Calories	616 kcal
Fat	37.5 g
Carbohydrates	50.6 g
Protein	21.9 g
Cholesterol	140 mg
Sodium	616 mg

Ingredients

1 skinless, boneless chicken breast half
1/2 C. couscous
1/2 C. water
1 tbsp unsalted butter
1 pinch salt
1 tbsp salted butter
1/4 C. capers, drained
3 dates, pitted and chopped

1/4 C. mascarpone cheese
1/4 C. heavy cream
salt and ground black pepper to taste (optional)
1 date, pitted and chopped
1/4 cucumber, diced
1/2 tomato, diced
1 tsp lemon juice (optional)

Directions

1. Set your outdoor grill for medium heat and lightly, grease the grill grate.
2. Cook the chicken breast on the grill for about 5-8 minutes per side.
3. Remove from the grill and cut the chicken breast in half.
4. In a pan, add the water, unsalted butter and a pinch of salt on high heat and bring to a boil.
5. Remove from the heat and stir in the couscous.
6. Keep aside, covered for about 10 minutes.
7. Uncover and with a fork, fluff the couscous.
8. In a skillet, melt the salted butter on medium heat.
9. Add the capers and 3 dates and gently, stir for a few times till the dates are heated.
10. Stir in the mascarpone cheese and cream and cook till the cheese and cream melts, stirring continuously.
11. Simmer for about 3 minutes, stirring continuously.
12. Stir in the mix with salt and pepper and remove from the heat.
13. In a serving platter, place the couscous and sprinkle with the chopped date.
14. Place 2 pieces of chicken breast over the couscous and top with the cheese sauce.
15. Garnish with the diced cucumber and tomato and serve with a drizzling of the lemon juice.

SIMPLE
Scones

Prep Time: 20 mins

Total Time: 32 mins

Servings per Recipe: 18
Calories   164 kcal
Fat   5.6 g
Carbohydrates   27.3g
Protein   3.7 g
Cholesterol   11 mg
Sodium   310 mg

Ingredients

2 C. whole-wheat flour
1 C. all-purpose flour
3 tbsp baking powder
1/4 tsp salt
1 tbsp sugar
1 tsp cinnamon
1/3 C. cold butter

3/4 C. chopped dates
1/2 C. chocolate chips
1 1/2 C. milk
milk for brushing
extra sugar and cinnamon to sprinkle

Directions

1. Set your oven to 400 degrees F before doing anything else and lightly, grease a baking sheet.
2. In a large bowl, sift together the flours, baking powder, salt, sugar and cinnamon.
3. Rub the butter into the flour mixture till a fine breadcrumbs like mixture forms.
4. Stir in the dates and chocolate chips.
5. Add the milk and mix till a ball like dough forms.
6. Place the dough onto a floured surface and roll into about 1/2-inch thick circle.
7. With a floured round cookie cutter, cut the dough into round scones.
8. Arrange the scones onto the prepared baking sheet in a single layer.
9. Coat the scones with the milk and sprinkle with the cinnamon and sugar mixture.
10. Cook in the oven for about 10-12 minutes.

Complex
Oven Dates

🍲 Prep Time: 20 mins
🕐 Total Time: 1 hr

Servings per Recipe: 16
Calories   225 kcal
Fat   7.6 g
Carbohydrates   37.7g
Protein   4.4 g
Cholesterol   6 mg
Sodium   55 mg

Ingredients

1 C. toasted pine nuts
1/2 C. white wine
1/4 C. honey
1/2 C. crumbled Gorgonzola cheese
2 C. dates - pitted and cut lengthwise to the center
ground black pepper to taste

salt to taste
1 C. honey, warmed
1/2 C. slivered, toasted almonds

Directions

1. In a bowl, mix together the pine nuts, white wine and 1/4 C. of the honey and keep aside for at least 30 minutes.
2. Drain well.
3. Set your oven to 350 degrees F and grease a baking dish.
4. In a bowl, mix together the Gorgonzola cheese and pine nuts.
5. Season the inside of each date with the black pepper.
6. Place the Gorgonzola mixture in the dates and sprinkle the outside with the salt.
7. Place the stuffed dates into the prepared baking dish in a single layer and top with 1 C. of the honey.
8. Cook in the oven for about 10 minutes.
9. Serve the cooked dates with a garnishing of the almonds.

A SIMPLE
Candy

🥣 Prep Time: 10 mins
🕐 Total Time: 8 hr 30 mins

Servings per Recipe: 10
Calories	334 kcal
Fat	13 g
Carbohydrates	56.1g
Protein	2.3 g
Cholesterol	14 mg
Sodium	43 mg

Ingredients

2 C. white sugar
1 C. milk
1/4 C. butter
1 C. chopped dates
1 C. chopped pecans
1 tsp vanilla extract

Directions

1. In a pan, add the milk and butter and bring to a boil, without stirring.
2. Cook for about 20 minutes or till the temperature of the mixture reaches to 250 degrees F.
3. Immediately, remove from the heat and stir in the dates, pecans and vanilla.
4. Wet a cheesecloth piece in water completely and arrange onto a smooth surface.
5. Place the candy mixture in the center of the cloth and roll the cloth around it to make a log.
6. Refrigerate for about 8 hours to overnight.
7. Remove the cloth and cut the log into the slice.

Full
Canadian Granola

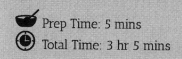 Prep Time: 5 mins

Total Time: 3 hr 5 mins

Servings per Recipe: 6

Calories	417 kcal
Fat	16.6 g
Carbohydrates	63.8g
Protein	8.2 g
Cholesterol	0 mg
Sodium	103 mg

Ingredients

6 tbsp applesauce
1/4 C. pure maple syrup
2 tbsp brown sugar (optional)
1 tsp ground cinnamon
1/4 tsp salt
1/4 tsp vanilla extract
1/4 tsp maple extract

1 tbsp hemp seed hearts (optional)
1 tbsp chia seeds (optional)
3 C. rolled oats
1 C. chopped pecans
1 C. Medjool dates, pitted and chopped

Directions

1. In a slow cooker, add the applesauce, maple syrup, brown sugar, and cinnamon, salt, vanilla extract, maple extract, hemp hearts and chia seeds and stir till well combined.
2. Stir in the oats and pecans.
3. Set the slow cooker on High and cover, venting the lid slightly.
4. Cook for about 3 hours, stirring occasionally.
5. Transfer the granola onto a parchment paper lined baking sheet and keep aside to cool completely.
6. This granola can be preserved in an airtight container.

HEAVY
Date Dip

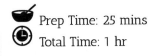

Prep Time: 25 mins

Total Time: 1 hr

Servings per Recipe: 48
Calories	65 kcal
Fat	2.1 g
Carbohydrates	11.8g
Protein	0.7 g
Cholesterol	9 mg
Sodium	47 mg

Ingredients

1 C. all-purpose flour
1 tsp baking powder
1/2 tsp salt
6 tbsp butter
1/3 C. white sugar
1 egg
1 tsp vanilla extract

1/4 C. heavy cream
3 C. whole pitted dates

Directions

1. Set your oven to 375 degrees F before doing anything else and grease 2 baking sheets.
2. In a bowl, sift together the flour, baking powder and salt.
3. In another bowl, add the butter and sugar and with an electric, beat on medium speed till light and fluffy.
4. Add egg and vanilla extract and beat till well combined.
5. Add the flour mixture in 3 additions, alternating with cream and mix till a thick mixture forms.
6. Dip each date in the mixture and arrange onto the prepared baking sheet.
7. Cook in the oven for about 10 minutes.

John the Juicer's
Smoothie

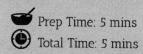

Prep Time: 5 mins

Total Time: 5 mins

Servings per Recipe: 1

Calories	400 kcal
Fat	17.6 g
Carbohydrates	59.6 g
Protein	8.5 g
Cholesterol	0 mg
Sodium	90 mg

Ingredients

1 ripe banana
1/2 C. cold unsweetened almond milk
1/3 C. frozen blueberries
2 dates, pitted and chopped
1 1/2 tbsp flax seeds
1 tbsp cashew butter

Directions

1. In a blender, add all the ingredients and pulse till smooth.

SEATTLE SWEET
Zucchini Bars

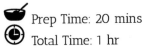 Prep Time: 20 mins

Total Time: 1 hr

Servings per Recipe: 48
Calories	109 kcal
Fat	5.2 g
Carbohydrates	15.1g
Protein	1.4 g
Cholesterol	8 mg
Sodium	83 mg

Ingredients

3/4 C. margarine, softened
1/2 C. white sugar
1/2 C. packed brown sugar
2 eggs
1 tsp vanilla extract
1 3/4 C. all-purpose flour
1/2 tsp salt
1 1/2 tsp baking powder
3/4 C. flaked coconut

3/4 C. chopped pitted dates
3/4 C. raisins
2 C. grated zucchini
1 tbsp margarine, melted
2 tbsp milk
1 tsp vanilla extract
1/4 tsp ground cinnamon
1 C. confectioners' sugar
1 C. finely chopped walnuts

Directions

1. Set your oven to 350 degrees F before doing anything else and lightly, grease a 13x9-inch baking dish.
2. In a large bowl, add the butter, white sugar, and brown sugar and beat till creamy.
3. Add the eggs and 1 tsp of the vanilla and beat till fluffy.
4. In another bowl, sift together the flour, salt and baking powder.
5. Add the flour mixture into the creamed mixture and mix well.
6. Stir in the coconut, dates, raisins and zucchini.
7. Transfer the mixture into the prepared baking dish evenly.
8. Cook in the oven for about 35-40 minutes.
9. Remove from the oven and keep onto the wire rack to cool in the pan for about 5-10 minutes.
10. For the icing in a bowl, add the melted margarine, milk, 1 tsp of the vanilla, cinnamon and confectioners' sugar and mix till well combined.
11. Spread the icing over the warm bars and sprinkle with the chopped walnuts.
12. Keep aside to cool completely.
13. Cut into equal sized bars and serve.

Moo-Moo
Bread

🥣 Prep Time: 30 mins

🕐 Total Time: 1 hr 30 mins

Servings per Recipe: 20

Calories	233 kcal
Fat	5.3 g
Carbohydrates	44.9 g
Protein	3.4 g
Cholesterol	19 mg
Sodium	212 mg

Ingredients

3 C. all-purpose flour
2 tsp baking powder
2 tsp baking soda
1/4 tsp salt
2 C. white sugar
1/4 C. shortening
2 eggs

1/2 tsp vanilla extract
1/2 C. chopped walnuts
1 1/2 C. chopped pitted dates
1 3/4 C. hot brewed coffee

Directions

1. Set your oven to 350 degrees F before doing anything else and grease and flour 28x4-inch) loaf pans.
2. In a bowl, sift together the flour, baking powder, baking soda and salt.
3. In another large bowl, add the sugar and shortening and beat till creamy.
4. Add the eggs and vanilla and beat till well combined.
5. Add the walnuts and dates into the flour mixture and toss to coat well.
6. Add the flour mixture into the sugar mixture, alternating with the hot coffee and mix well.
7. Place the mixture into the prepared loaf pans evenly.
8. Cook in the oven for about 1 hour or till a toothpick inserted in the center comes out clean.

Made in the USA
Las Vegas, NV
14 November 2020